CAMBRIDGE
UNIVERSITY PRESS

CAMBRIDGE ENGLISI
Language Assessment
Part of the University of Cambridge

CU00705273

Kid's Box for Ecuador

Updated Second Edition

Student's Book 1B

American English

Caroline Nixon & Michael Tomlinson

Ecuadorian CLIL content by Kate Cory-Wright and Jill Hadfield

Thanks and Acknowledgments

Authors' thanks

Many thanks to everyone at Cambridge University Press and in particular to:

Rosemary Bradley for supervising the whole project and for her keen editorial eye;
Emily Hird for her energy, enthusiasm, and enormous organizational capacity;
Colin Sage for his hard work, good ideas, and helpful suggestions;
Claire Appleyard for her editorial contribution.

Many thanks to Karen Elliot for her expertise and enthusiasm in the writing of the Phonics sections.

We would also like to thank all our pupils and colleagues at Star English, El Palmar, Murcia, and especially Jim Kelly and Julie Woodman for their help and suggestions at various stages of the project.

Dedications

I would like to dedicate this book to the women who have been my pillars of strength: Milagros Marín, Sara de Alba, Elia Navarro, and Maricarmen Balsalobre - CN

To Paloma, for her love, encouragement, and unwavering support. Thanks. - MT

The Authors and Publishers would like to thank the following teachers for their help in reviewing the material and for the invaluable feedback they provided:

Luciana Pittondo, Soledad Gimenez, Argentina; Gan Ping, Zou Yang, China; Keily Duran, Colombia; Elvia Gutierrez Reyes, Yadira Hernandez, Mexico; Rachel Lunan, Russia; Lorraine Mealing, Sharon Hopkins, Spain; Inci Kartal, Turkey.

The authors and publishers would like to thank the following consultants for their invaluable input:

Coralyn Bradshaw, Helen Chilton, Marla Del Signore, Pippa Mayfield, Hilary Ratcliff, Lynne Rushton, Melanie Williams.

We would also like to thank all the teachers who allowed us to observe their classes and who gave up their invaluable time for interviews and focus groups.

The authors and publishers acknowledge the following sources of copyright material and are grateful for the permissions granted. While every effort has been made, it has not always been possible to identify the sources of all the material used or to trace all copyright holders. If any omissions are brought to our notice, we will be happy to include the appropriate acknowledgments on reprinting.

t = top, c = center, b = below, l = left, r = right

p. 60 (tl): Shutterstock.com/Gualtiero Boffi; p. 60 (tr, bc): Shutterstock/Eric Isselee; p. 60 (bl): Getty Images/iStock/GlobalP; p. 60 (br): Shutterstock/ Ekaterina V. Borisova; p. 60 (tc): Shutterstock/defpicture; p. 61 (t): Thinkstock; p. 61a (tl): Getty Images/David Hiser/ The Image Bank; p. 61a (tc): Getty Images/Juergen Ritterbach/ DigitalVision; p. 61a (tr): Getty Images/Lilly Husbands; p. 61a (bl): Getty Images/onairda/iStock; p. 61a (bc): Getty Images/ Istvan Kadar Photography/Moment; p. 61a (br): Getty Images/ Ben Queenborough/Oxford Scientific; p. 61b (br): Getty Images/ Guy Edwardes/The Image Bank; p. 61b (tr): Getty Images/ KalypsoWorldPhotography/iStock; p. 61b (tl): Getty Images/Julia Davila-Lampe/Moment Open; p. 62 (l): Shutterstock/MIMOHE; p. 62 (r): Shutterstock/Jiri Foltyn; p. 62 (cl): Shutterstock/ Jassam; p. 62 (cr): Getty Images/The Image Bank/James Warwick; p. 76 (tl): Getty Images/AFP/TORU YAMANAKA;. 76 (cl): Alamy/©Kuttig - People; p. 76 (br): Corbis/ZUMA Press/©Brian Baer; p. 76 (bl): Corbis/©Onne van der Wal; p 76 (tr): Superstock/Juniors; p. 77 (t): Thinkstock; p. 77a (tl): Getty Images/Jupiterimages/Taxi; p. 77a (tr): Alamy/Supparsorn Wantarnagon; p. 77a (bl): Getty Images/Simon Watson/ The Image Bank; p. 77a (br): Getty Images/IMAGEMORE Co, Ltd.; p. 90 (tr, bl): SuperStock/Christie's Images Ltd; p. 90 (tl): Superstock/Leslie Hinrichs; p. 90 (br): Superstock/Peter Willi; p. 91 (t): Thinkstock. We would like to thank the Crow family for the paintings *Tren Volador* (p. 91a) and *Lluvia de manzanas* (p. 91b).

Cover photography by Julie Watson.

Background image on pages 61a, 61b, 77a, 77b, 91a, 91b by Getty Images/madebymarco/iStock.

Commissioned photography on pages 52, 68, 81 by Trevor Clifford Photography.

The authors and publishers are grateful to the following illustrators:

Beatrice Costamagna, c/o Pickled ink; Chris Garbutt, c/o Arena; Lucía Serrano Guerroro; Andrew Hennessey; Kelly Kennedy, c/o Syvlie Poggio; Sara Lynn, c/o Astound; Rob McKlurkan, c/o The Bright Agency; Andrew Painter; Melanie Sharp, c/o Syvlie Poggio; Marie Simpson, c/o Pickled ink; Christos Skaltsas (hyphen); Emily Skinner, c/o Graham-Cameron Illustration; Lisa Smith; Gary Swift; Ando Twin, c/o Astound; Lisa Williams, c/o Syvlie Poggio;

The publishers are grateful to the following contributors:

Louise Edgeworth: art direction
Hilary Fletcher: picture research
Wild Apple Design Ltd: page design
Blooberry: additional design
Melanie Sharp: cover illustration
John Green and Tim Woolf, TEFL Audio: audio recordings
John Marshall Media, Inc. and Lisa Hutchins: audio recordings for the American English edition
Robert Lee: song writing
hyphen S.A.: publishing management, American English edition

Language summary

	Key vocabulary	Key grammar and functions	Phonics
7 Wild animals page 48	**Animals:** crocodile, elephant, giraffe, hippo, monkey, snake, tiger **Body parts:** arm, foot/feet, hand, leg, tail	They have (big mouths). They don't have (tails). Do they have (long legs)? How many (teeth) do they have?	Short vowel sound: "i" (six)
8 My clothes page 54	**Clothes:** jacket, (pair of) pants, shoes, skirt, socks, T-shirt	He/She has (red pants). He/She doesn't have (a jacket).	Short vowel sound: "o" (doll)

	Key vocabulary	Key grammar and functions	Phonics
9 Fun time! page 64	**Activities:** play soccer / basketball / tennis, play the guitar/piano, swim, ride a bike, sing, fish	I/You/She/He can (sing). I/You/She/He can't (drive a car). What can you do? Can you (fish)?	Consonant sound: "l" (Lily, blue)
10 At the amusement park page 70	**Vehicles:** boat, bus, helicopter, motorcycle, plane, ship, truck	What are you doing? I'm (flying).	Short vowel sound: "u" (duck)

	Key vocabulary	Key grammar and functions	Phonics
11 Our house page 78	**Rooms:** bathroom, bedroom, dining room, hallway, kitchen, living room **Activities:** eat fish, watch TV, take a bath	What's he/she doing? He's/She's (listening to music). What are they doing? They're (sitting on the couch). Is he/she (reading)? Yes, he/she is. No, he/she isn't. **Verb + -ing spellings:** coloring, playing	Initial consonant sound: "h" (horse)
12 Party time! page 84	**Food:** apple, banana, burger, cake, chocolate, ice cream, kiwi **Activities:** make a cake	I like (cake). I don't like (chocolate). Do you like (snakes)? Yes, I do. No, I don't.	Long vowel sound: "i_e"/ "y" (bike, fly)

1 CD3 Listen and point.

giraffe

elephant

snake

crocodile

monkey

hippo

tiger

2 CD3 Listen and repeat.

3 ▶5 CD3 ⚹ Say the chant. Do the actions.

4 ▶6 CD3 ⚹ Listen and point. Answer.

Vocabulary

crocodile   elephant   giraffe   hippo   monkey   snake   tiger

5 🔊7 CD3 👂 Listen and point.

foot

hand

leg

arm

tail

feet

They have big ears.

6 🔊8 CD3 💬 Listen and repeat.

Grammar

They have / They don't have arms / feet / hands / legs / tails.

7 🔟 🎵 Sing the song.

8 Act it out and say.

What am I?   You're an elephant.

fish

big

Six big fish.

10 👥💬 Play the game. Ask and answer.

Do they have small ears?

No, they don't.

big	heads, ears, feet,
small	mouths

short	tails, noses,
long	legs, arms

11  Listen to the story.

12 Act out the story.

8 My clothes

1 🔊15 CD3 👆 Listen and point.

T-shirt

skirt

socks

shoes

jacket

pants

2 🔊16 CD3 💬 Listen and repeat.

54

3 18 CD3 💬 Say the chant.

4 19 CD3 💬 Listen and say the number.

1 2 3 4

Vocabulary

jacket pants shoes skirt socks T-shirt

5 21 CD3 Listen and point.

6 22 CD3 Listen and repeat.

Grammar

He/She has … He/She doesn't have …

7  Listen and correct.

8 Sing the song.

doll

socks   box

A d**o**ll in s**o**cks on a b**o**x.

10 **Ask and answer.**

She has a yellow jacket.

Eva!

11 🔊 **31** **CD3** Listen to the story.

12 🔊 **32** **CD3** 💬 Listen and say the number.

1 · 33 CD3 · Listen and point.

plain

river

forest

2 · Look and say.

Hippo?

River and plain.

Vocabulary

forest   plain   river

Now you!
Workbook page 60

3  **Listen to the story.**

1

2

3

4

4 **Listen. Say "happy" or "sad."**

1 🔍💬 Look and say.

jaguar

iguana

monkey

llama

condor

pelican

2 🧍💬 Play the game. Ask and guess.

They have four legs.

Do they have short tails?

Yes!

A llama!

3 🔍💬 Look and say.

Coast

Amazon

Andes

COLOMBIA

ECUADOR

QUITO

Guayaquil

PERU

4 👂✋ Listen and point.

5 🔍💬 Look and say the three animals.

6 ✏️ Draw your own animal.

Review

1 🔊 36 CD3 💬 Listen and say the number.

2 🔍 💬 Look, read, and match.

> It's a hippo.

zebra	hippo	elephant	crocodile

3  Play the game. Say the words.

9 Fun time!

play the piano

play tennis

play soccer

play basketball

play the guitar

swim

ride a bike

2 [39] CD3 Listen and repeat.

64

3 **41** CD3 💬 Listen and answer.

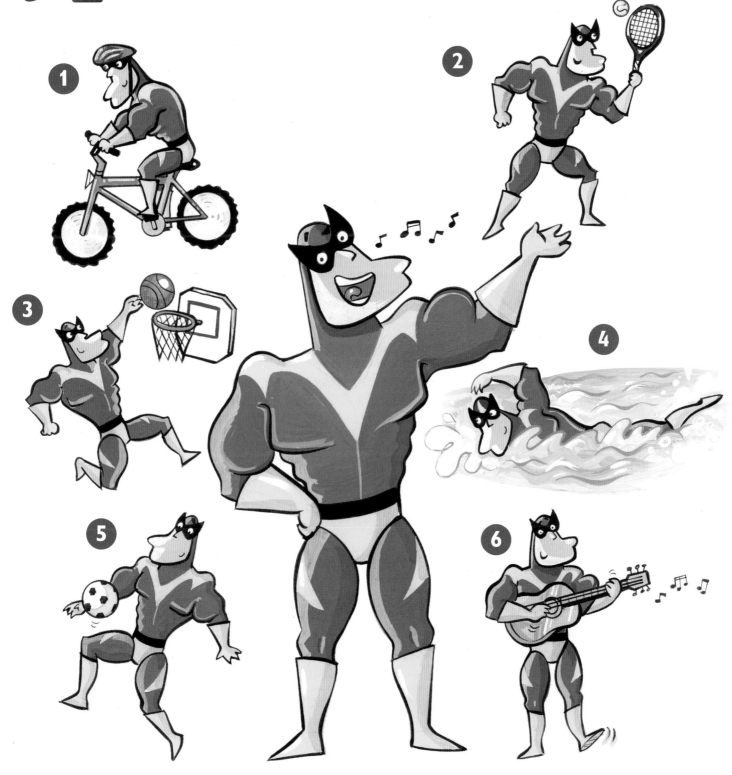

4 **42** CD3 🎵 Sing the song.

Vocabulary

play basketball / soccer / tennis   play the guitar/piano   swim   ride a bike

5 44 CD3 Listen and point.

6 45 CD3 Listen and repeat.

Grammar
I/You/He/She can …   I/You/He/She can't …

7  Say the chant.

8 Listen and answer.

Who can draw? Grandma.

Lily

blue

Lily has a blue and yellow tail.

10 💬 Ask and answer.

Can you sing?

Yes, I can.

Can you swim?

No, I can't.

11 🔊 **51** CD3 Listen to the story.

12 😎💬 Act out the story.

10 At the amusement park

1 CD4 2 Listen and point.

truck

motorcycle

plane

boat

bus

helicopter

2 CD4 3 Listen and repeat.

3   Say the chant. Do the actions.

4   Listen and answer.

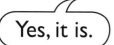

Is the red car in the shoe? — Yes, it is.

Vocabulary

boat   bus   helicopter   motorcycle   plane   truck   ship

5 Listen and point.

6 Listen and repeat.

Grammar
What are you doing? I'm driving / flying / riding / walking.

7 Sing the song.

8 Do the actions. Play the game.

What am I doing?   You're driving a truck.

9 ▶13 CD4 💬 Monty's phonics

duck

under

bus

The ducks are under the bus.

10 ▶14 CD4 💬 Listen and correct.

> I'm driving my car.

> No, you're walking.

1

2

3

4

5

6

11 **Listen to the story.**

12 **Listen and say the number.**

Marie's sports Things for sports

1 🔊18 CD4 💬 Listen and say.

> They're sailing.

| playing basketball | playing Ping-Pong |
| riding bikes | riding horses | sailing |

1

2

3

4

5

2 💬 Say and answer.

> They have a big orange ball.

> They're playing basketball.

Vocabulary
play Ping-Pong   sail

Now you!
Workbook page 76

3 🔊 **19** **CD4** Listen to the story.

4 🔊 **20** **CD4** 💬 Listen and say the number. Act it out.

Functions

I can help you.   Work in teams.

1 👂 ✋ Listen and point.

clap　hop　jump rope　play marbles

2 👂 Listen and do the actions.

3 👤💬 Play the game. Ask and answer.

> What's the girl doing?

> She's hopping.

Language through the arts

4 💬👤 Play the game. Use a spinner.

> It's your turn.

> Hop five times!

> It's my turn.

> Jump rope three times!

1

2

3

4

5

11 Our house

1 **21** CD4 Listen and point.

bedroom

bathroom

living room

dining room

kitchen

hallway

2 **22** CD4 Listen and repeat.

3 **24** **CD4** Listen and correct.

Monty's in the bathroom.

No, he isn't. He's in the bedroom.

4 **25** **CD4** Listen and answer.

Where's the computer?

It's in the kitchen.

Vocabulary

bathroom   bedroom   dining room   hallway   kitchen   living room

5 **26** CD4 **Listen and point.**

What's Scott doing?

He's drawing a picture.

6 **27** CD4 **Listen and repeat.**

80

Grammar

What's he/she doing?   He's/She's ...ing

7 ♫ Sing the song.

8 💬 Ask and answer.

What's Sally doing?

She's reading a book.

Where is she?

She's in the bedroom.

horse

hippo   A horse and a hippo in a helicopter.

10 Say and guess.

| playing | driving | flying | eating |
| reading | playing | swimming | watching |

They're eating fish.

Number four.

 1

 2

 3

 4

 5

 6

 7

 8

 Listen to the story.

  Listen and say "yes" or "no."

12 Party time!

1 🔊 35 CD4 👂 Listen and point.

ice cream

apple

banana

cake

burger

chocolate

2 🔊 36 CD4 💬 Listen and repeat.

3 38 CD4 💬 Say the chant.

4 39 CD4 💬 Listen and say "yes" or "no."

Vocabulary

apple   banana   burger   cake   chocolate   ice cream   kiwi   orange

Grammar
I like ...   I don't like ...   Do you like ... ?

7 ♪ Sing the song.

8 💬 Ask and answer.

Do you like apples?	Yes, I do.
Do you like ice cream?	No, I don't.

pie

like

bike

white

I like my white bike!

10 47 CD4 💬 Read. Listen and say the name.

Sam I like and , but I don't like 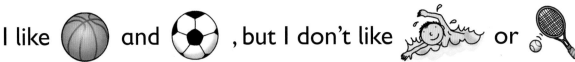 or .

Sue I don't like or , but I like and .

May I like and , but I don't like 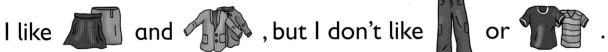 or .

Ben I don't like or , but I like and .

11 🔊 **49 CD4** Listen to the story.

12 🎭💬 Act out the story.

1 👂💬 Point and say the food.

2 🔊50 CD4 💬 Listen and say the number.

Now you!
Workbook page 90

3   Listen and point.

4   Say the chant. Do the actions.

Vocabulary

brush your teeth   wash apples   wash your hands

1 🎧✏️ Listen and point.

> apples falling flying looking
> mountains people sky train

1

2 🎧💬 Listen and correct.

The mountains are gray and black.

No. The mountains are green.

3 💬 Spot the differences.

2

The mountains are green.

No. The mountains are gray and black.

Language through the arts

4 ✏️ Draw your own magic picture.

Vocabulary

falling flying looking mountain people sky

Review

1 🔊 53 CD4 💬 Listen and answer.

2 🔍 Read.

I'm Ben. I'm **7**. I like ⚽ and 🏐, but I don't like 🏓. I can 🏊 and ride a 🚲, but I can't play the 🎸. I like 🍰 and 🍔, but I don't like 🍫 or 🍦. I like 🍎 and 🥝. I'm eating a 🍌 now.

The elephant's drinking water.

Grammar reference

7

They have big mouths.	They don't have tails.
Do they have long legs?	

8

She has your red pants.	He doesn't have a white ball.
Does he/she have a train?	Yes, he/she does. No, he/she doesn't.

doesn't = does not

9

I ...	can can't	sing. play the guitar.
Can you ride a bike?		

can't = cannot

10

What are you doing?	I'm flying.
Are you flying your helicopter?	

11

What's he/she doing? What are they doing?	He's/She's listening to music. They're sitting on the couch.
Is he/she listening to music?	Yes, he/she is. No, he/she isn't.

what's = what is

12

I like cake.	I don't like chocolate.
Do you like snakes?	Yes, I do. No, I don't.

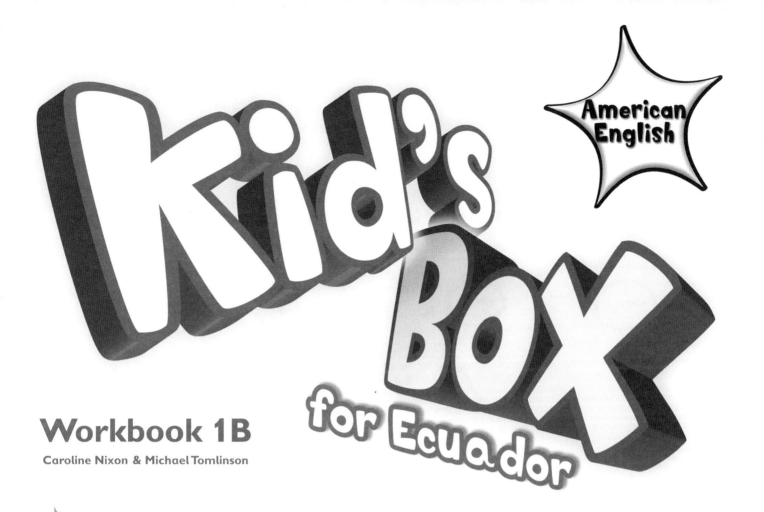

Kid's Box for Ecuador

American English

Workbook 1B

Caroline Nixon & Michael Tomlinson

1 🔊 ✏️ Listen and connect the dots.

2 ✏️ Read and draw lines. ↓ ↘ →

①

doll	bike	ball
nine	hippo	bag
table	seven	eight

②

elephant	ten	crocodile
chair	seven	car
computer	five	bag

③

pencil	ball	bag
tiger	eraser	one
doll	five	book

④

bike	two	door
three	doll	train
snake	monkey	giraffe

3 🔍✏️ Read and answer. Write "yes" or "no."

1. Are the giraffes sad? ..... *no* .....

2. Are the elephants happy? ....

3. Are the crocodiles long? ....

4. Are the snakes short? ....

4 ✏️ Color the animals.

💬✏️ Now ask and answer. Color your friend's animals.

My giraffes are purple.

5  Listen and write the number.

6 Read and check (✓) or put an X.

Animals	hands	arms	legs	feet	tails
snakes	X	X	X	X	✓
monkeys					
birds					
elephants					
crocodiles					
fish					
tigers					
zebras					

7 Look and read. Write "yes" or "no."

The elephants have small ears.   _no_

(1) The monkeys are on bikes.   _____

(2) The giraffes are under the elephants.   _____

(3) The small giraffe is fat.   _____

(4) The tigers are next to the crocodiles.   _____

(5) The snakes have eyes.   _____

8 🔊 13 CD3 ✏️ Listen and write "a," "e," or "i."

① l <u>e</u> g

② f___sh

③ bl___ck

④ b___g

⑤ h___ppo

⑥ p___n

⑦ s___ster

⑧ h___nd

9 ✏️ Draw and write.

Me!

My favorite wild animals are _____ .
They're _____ .
They have _____ .

52

My picture dictionary

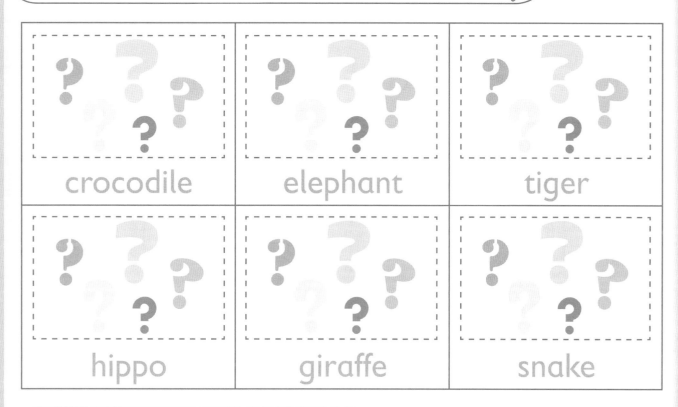

crocodile	elephant	tiger
hippo	giraffe	snake

My star card

 Can you say these words?

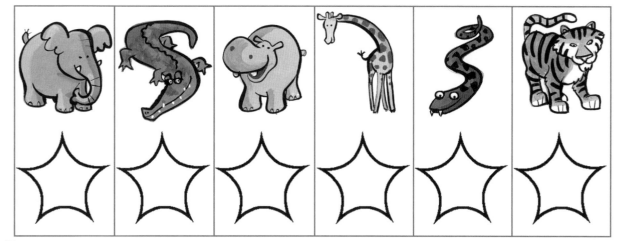

Color the stars.

8 My clothes

1 🔍 ✏️ Find and circle the number.

🧦	1	2	3	4	5	6	7	8	9	(10)
👕	1	2	3	4	5	6	7	8	9	10
👗	1	2	3	4	5	6	7	8	9	10
👟	1	2	3	4	5	6	7	8	9	10
🧥	1	2	3	4	5	6	7	8	9	10
👖	1	2	3	4	5	6	7	8	9	10

2 🔊17 CD3 💬 Listen and answer.

3  Listen and color.

4 Draw and write.

Me!

My favorite clothes are my _____.

5 **23** CD3 Listen and color.

Sue

Nick

Kim

Tony

May

6 **24** CD3 Listen and match.

7 Read the question. Listen and write a name or a number. There are two examples.

3   ~~Kim~~   Tom   ~~10~~   8   Bill   9

What is the name of the girl? _____Kim_____

How old is she? _____10_____

1 What is the name of the dog? _____

2 How old is the dog? _____

3 What is the name of Kim's brother? _____

4 How old is Kim's brother? _____

5 How many children are in Kim's class? _____

8 🔊 ✏️ **Listen and write "a," "e," "i," or "o."**

1 d o ll

2 c __ p

3 d __ g

4 p __ n

5 f __ sh

6 s __ ck

7 b __ x

8 s __ x

9 ✏️ **Write the sentences.**

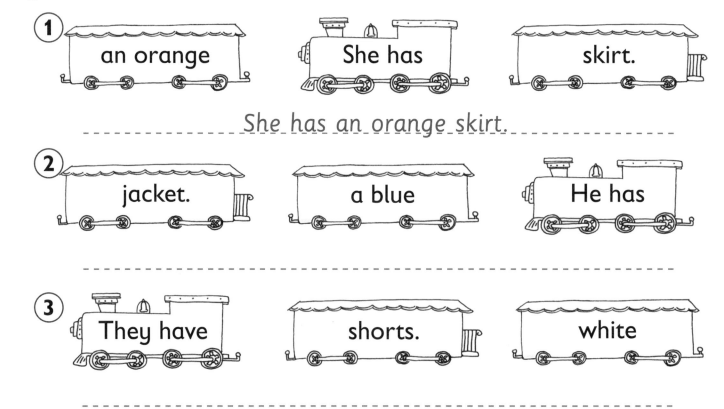

1 an orange She has skirt.

She has an orange skirt.

2 jacket. a blue He has

3 They have shorts. white

My picture dictionary ⭐

jacket	shoes	skirt
socks	pants	T-shirt

My star card ⭐

 Can you say these words?

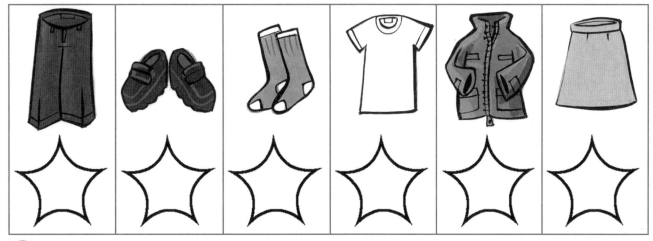

Color the stars.

1 Read and check (✓) or put an ✗.

	river	plain	forest
fish 🐟	✓	✗	✗
giraffe			
hippo			
crocodile			

Now you! 2  Read. Write and draw.

~~plains~~ long gray elephant forests

This animal is from

_____plains_____ and

_____. It's big

and _____.

It has two big

ears and a very

_____ nose.

What is it? It's an

_____.

3 ✏️ Read and write the number.

1. The birds are sad. `4`

2. The river is dirty. ☐

3. The forest has trees. ☐

4. The river doesn't have fish. ☐

5. The forest doesn't have trees. ☐

6. The birds are happy. ☐

7. The river has fish. ☐

8. The river is clean. ☐

Review

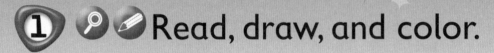

1 🔍 ✏️ Read, draw, and color.

Ben

Bill

Bill
long shoes
a dirty T-shirt
a big nose
a sad mouth
purple pants

Ben
short shoes
a happy mouth
green hair
a small nose
a red jacket

2 🔊 💬 Listen and say "Bill" or "Ben."

3 💬 Say the sentences.

Fish and snakes don't have legs.

🐟🐟	and	🐍🐍	no legs.
🐱🐱	and	🐶🐶	no hands.
🦓🦓	and	🦒🦒	no arms.
🐘🐘	and	🐊🐊	no hair.

 **Read and write.**

| arms | ears | ~~face~~ | hands | mouth | tail | two | two |

At the safari park

I'm small and brown. I have a funny ①___*face*___

with ②_____ big ③_____ and a big

④_____. My ⑤_____ are long and

I have ⑥_____

big ⑦_____. I have

a long ⑧_____.

9 Fun time!

1 🔊40 CD3 ✏️ **Listen and write the number.**

2 🔍 ✏️ **Read and match.**

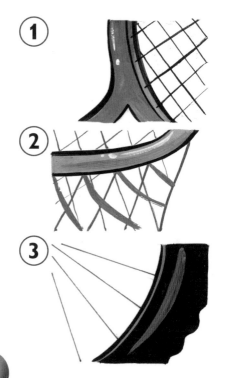

① ② ③

swim

play the guitar

play tennis

ride a bike

play soccer

play basketball

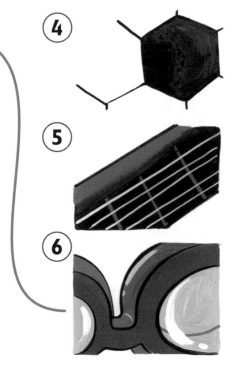

④ ⑤ ⑥

9

3 🔍✏️ Find six words.

① | ? | a | ? |

③ | ? |

② | ? | ? |

④

w	a	s	g	r	i	d	e
r	s	p	u	g	i	t	a
a	w	b	i	k	e	r	p
t	i	n	t	i	s	l	l
o	m	l	a	s	t	c	a
o	m	e	r	x	u	r	y
t	e	n	n	i	s	a	e

play the | ? |

4 ✏️ Write the words.

①  ②  ③  ④  ⑤  ⑥

soccer ~~guitar~~ play ride swim tennis

① play the __guitar__

② _____ basketball

③ play _____

④ play _____

⑤ _____ a bike

⑥ _____

5 🔊 46 CD3 ✏️ Listen and check (✓) or put an ✗.

① ☒
② ☐
③ ☐
④ ☐
⑤ ☐
⑥ ☐

6 ✏️ What can you do? Draw and write.

Me! ✓	✗
✓	✗
I can _____ .	I can't _____ .

7   Look and write the words.

Example

<u>b a s k e t b a l l</u>

b s k a t e
b l l a

Questions

1

_ _ _

r c a

2

_ _ _ _

k i b e

3

_ _ _ _ _

r s h o e

4

_ _ _ _ _ _

n i n e t s

5

_ _ _ _ _ _

t a g u i r

8 🎵 50 CD3 ✏️ Listen and circle "l" in the words.

① Li(l)y

② b l u e

③ s o c c e r b a l l

④ p e n c i l

⑤ p l a y

⑥ c l e a n

⑦ y e l l o w

⑧ p l a n e

9 ✏️ Write the words.

| ~~basketball~~ a bike draw soccer the guitar |
| a horse the piano sing swim tennis |

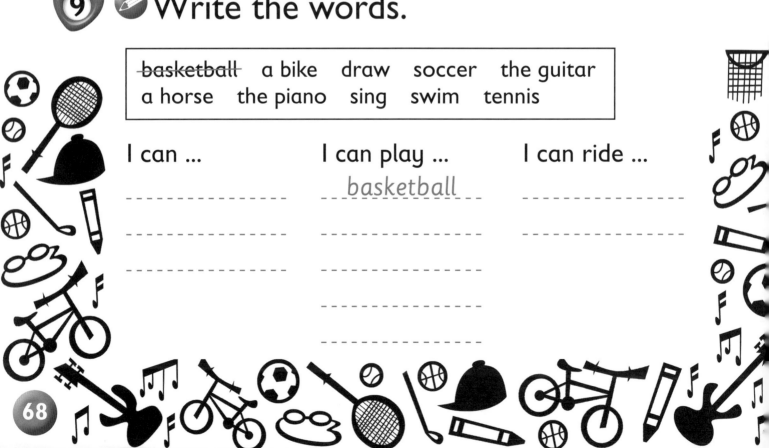

I can ...

_____

_____

_____

I can play ...
basketball

_____

_____

_____

_____

I can ride ...

_____

_____

My picture dictionary

play basketball	ride a bike	play tennis
swim	play soccer	play the guitar

My star card

 Can you say these words?

Color the stars.

10 At the amusement park

1 ✏️ **Write the words.**

bike boat bus car ~~helicopter~~
truck motorcycle plane train

①

②

③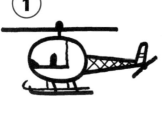

④

⑤

⑥

⑦

⑧

⑨

Crossword:

```
            ¹h
   ²□□□      e
            l
   ³□□□      i
            c
            o        ⁴□
            p
   ⁵□□       t    ⁶□□
            e
  ⁷□□⁸□□□    r □□□□□□
     □
   ⁹□□□
     □
     □
```

2 ▶ CD4 ✏️ **Listen and color.**

10

3 ✏️ **Draw stars.**

   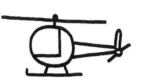

💬✏️ **Now ask and answer. Draw your friend's stars.**

(Where's the star?) (It's on the truck.)

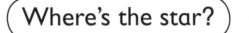 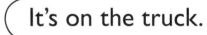

   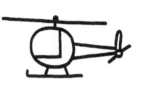

4 ✏️ **Write the words.**

~~truck~~   ~~T-shirt~~   helicopter   boat   pants   plane
skirt   jacket   shoes   motorcycle   socks   bus

truck

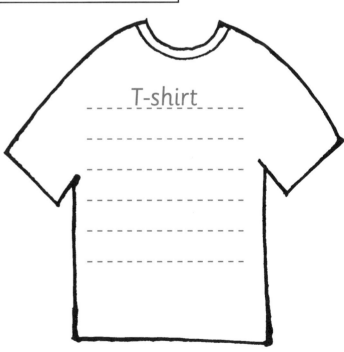

T-shirt

5 **9** CD4 ✏ Listen and draw colored lines.

6 ✏ Draw and write.

riding	horse	bike	motorcycle	driving	sitting
truck	bus	ship	flying	plane	helicopter

Me!

I'm _____ a _____ .

**Listen and check (✓) the box.
There is one example.**

Where's the truck?

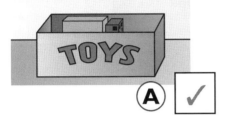 (A) ✓    (B) ☐   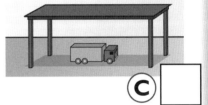 (C) ☐

(1) What's Anna doing?

 (A) ☐    (B) ☐    (C) ☐

(2) Which toy is under the chair?

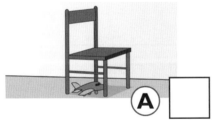 (A) ☐   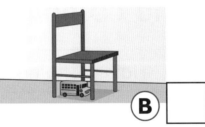 (B) ☐   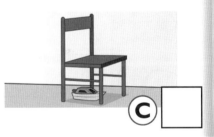 (C) ☐

(3) What color is Matt's motorcycle?

 (A) ☐    (B) ☐    (C) ☐

(4) Which boy is Alex?

 (A) ☐    (B) ☐     (C) ☐

8 🔵 ✏️ **Listen and write "a," "e," "i," "o," or "u."**

1. h_a_ppy
2. s__cks
3. b__s
4. s__ng
5. d__ck
6. f__sh
7. s__d
8. l__g

9 🔍 ✏️ **Read and complete.**

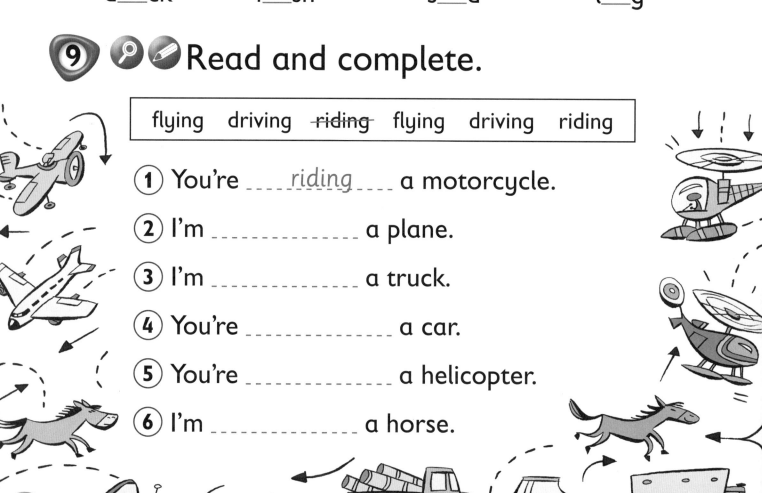

| flying | driving | ~~riding~~ | flying | driving | riding |

1. You're ___riding___ a motorcycle.
2. I'm _____ a plane.
3. I'm _____ a truck.
4. You're _____ a car.
5. You're _____ a helicopter.
6. I'm _____ a horse.

My picture dictionary

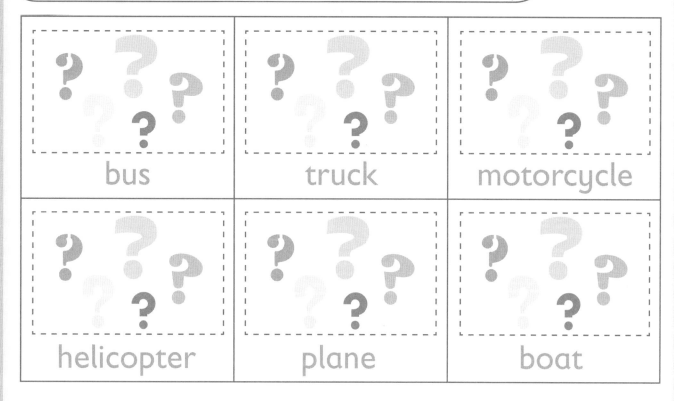

bus	truck	motorcycle
helicopter	plane	boat

My star card

Can you say these words?

Color the stars.

Now you! ①  ✏️💬 **Match and say.**

> She has a big ball.

①  ②  ③  ④  ⑤

| bike | big ball | small ball | boat | horse |

② 🔍✏️ **Match and write.**

| horse   boat   basketball   ~~bike~~   Ping-Pong |

① They're riding a ___bike___ .

② They're sitting on a _____ .

③ They're playing _____ .

④ They're playing _____ .

⑤ They're riding a _____ .

3 💬 ✏️ Work in teams. Color the boxes.

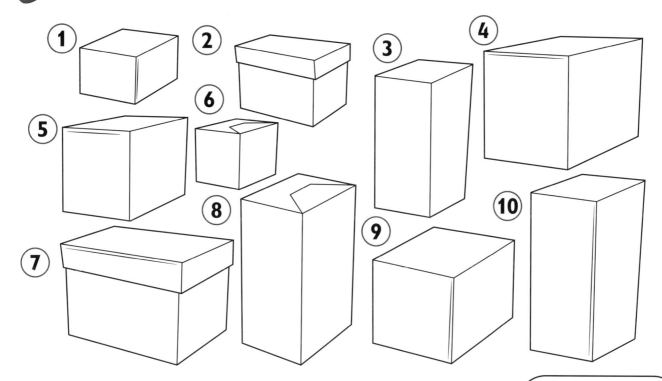

4 🧑 ✏️ Play the game in teams.

> Number one is yellow.

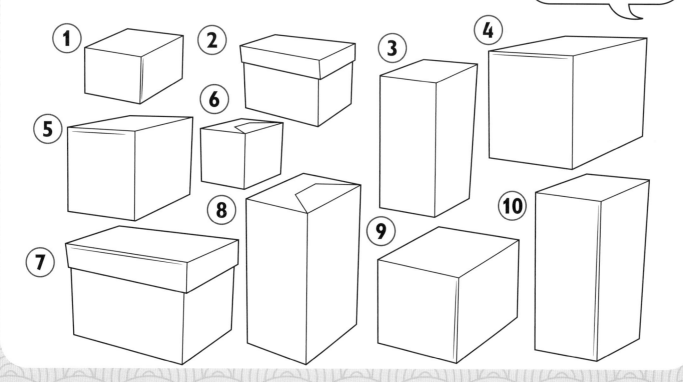

11 Our house

1 **23** **CD4** Listen and draw lines. There is one example.

Alex   Dan   Grace   Hugo

May   Bill   Sue

2 🔍✏️ Follow the lines and write.

~~bedroom~~	living room	kitchen	hallway

① ② ③ ④

bedroom _____ _____ _____

3 ✏️ Draw your house.

Me!

My house has

_____

_____

_____

_____

_____

_____

_____ .

4 🎧 28 CD4 ✏️ Listen and color the stars.

5 🔍 ✏️ Match and write.

(1) She's drawing a ____picture____ .

(2) He's reading a _____ .

(3) She's sitting on a _____ .

(4) They're listening to _____ .

(5) He's driving a _____ .

(6) They're playing _____ .

 chair

 tennis

 car

 book

 music

 picture

6 Look, read, and write.

Where are the children?   in the _____ kitchen _____

How many people are there?   _____ two _____

(1) What's the girl eating?   some _____

(2) What does the boy have?   a _____

(3) What's the girl doing?   listening to _____

(4) What animal can the boy see?   an _____

(5) Who's pointing?   the _____

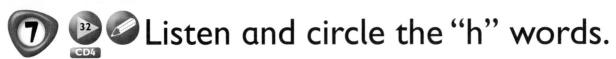

7 🎵32 CD4 ✏️ Listen and circle the "h" words.

① ② ③ ④

⑤ ⑥ ⑦ ⑧ ⑨

8 ✏️ Complete the sentences.

eating	~~listening~~	reading	taking

① He's __listening__ to music.   ② She's _____ a bath.

③ He's _____ a fish.   ④ She's _____ a book.

My picture dictionary

living room

bedroom

kitchen

bathroom

hallway

dining room

My star card

💬 Can you say these words?

✏️ Color the stars.

12 Party time!

1  Listen and color.

2 Circle and write the words.

a	w	e	i	f	i	s	h	s
c	h	o	c	o	l	a	t	e
a	b	r	e	c	k	f	a	m
k	l	t	c	h	e	j	p	r
e	b	u	r	g	e	r	p	o
p	r	o	e	v	i	s	l	b
b	a	n	a	n	a	t	e	g
j	z	o	m	e	r	s	t	u
o	r	a	n	g	e	v	i	e

① _ _ _ _ _ _ _ _ _ _

② _ _ _ _ _ _ _ _ _ _

③ _ _ _ _ _ _ _ _ _ _

④  _ _ _ _ _ _ _ _ _ _

⑤ _ _ _ _ _ _ _ _ _ _

⑥ *ice cream*

⑦ _ _ _ _ _ _ _ _ _ _

⑧ _ _ _ _ _ _ _ _ _ _

12

3 Write the words.

1. → *cat*

2. →

3. →

4. →

4 Read and complete.

young

~~eating~~

banana

cake

The small monkey's __*eating*__ an orange, and the big monkey has some _____. The old monkey's eating a _____, and the _____ monkey has ice cream.

5 **42** **CD4** **Listen and check (✓) or put an X.**

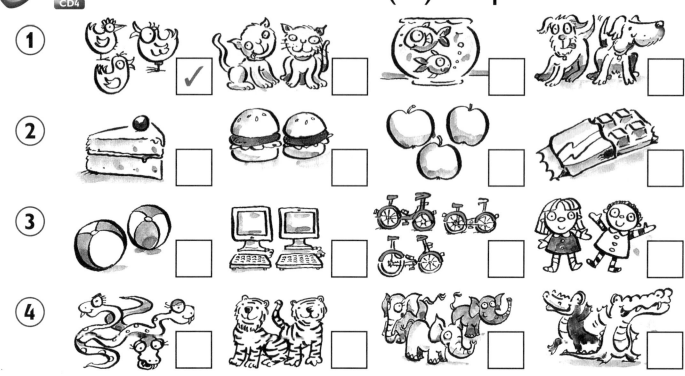

6 **Write "like" or "don't like."**

I _ _ _ _ _ _ _ _ _ fish.

I _ _ _ _ _ _ _ _ _ burgers.

I _ _ _ _ _ _ _ _ _ ice cream.

I _ _ _ _ _ _ _ _ _ apples.

Listen and color. There is one example.

8   Listen and write the words.

| bike | white | drive | nine | ~~like~~ | five |

1

_____ like _____

2 **5**

_____

3

_____

4 **9**

_____

5

_____

6

_____

9 Check (✓) the boxes.

Name						
Me						

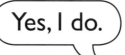 Now ask and answer in groups.

Do you like apples?   Yes, I do.

My picture dictionary

apple	banana	burger
cake	chocolate	ice cream

My star card

 Can you say these words?

Color the stars.

1 Read and circle a word.

This is Fred Food.

His nose is a banana / an ice-cream cone.

His mouth is a fish / a burger.

His ears are apples / oranges.

His hair is grapes / kiwis.

His eyes are cakes / burgers.

Now you! **2**  Draw and color your Fred Food.

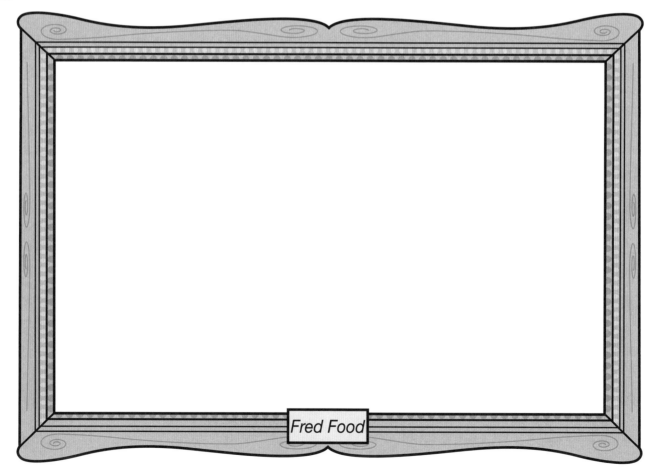

Fred Food

3 🔍✏️ **Order the pictures.**

1

 `2`
 `3`
 `1`

2

3

4 🔍✏️ **Read and write.**

| brushing   washing   washing |

He's _____
his hands.

She's _____
her teeth.

He's _____
his apples.

Review

9 10 11 12

1 ✏️ Check (✓) a box.

reading a book						
eating fish						
watching TV						
taking a bath						

💬 ✏️ **Now ask and answer. Check (✓) your friend's box.**

What's the old monster doing?   He's eating fish.

reading a book						
eating fish						
watching TV						
taking a bath						

2 ✏️ Circle the different word.

①　kiwi　　　　　apple　　　　orange　　　　(guitar)

②　truck　　　　ice cream　　train　　　　bus

③　burger　　　tiger　　　　giraffe　　　crocodile

④　bathroom　　kitchen　　　bedroom　　chocolate

⑤　motorcycle　helicopter　truck　　　　hallway

⑥　play　　　　swim　　　　bike　　　　ride

3 🔍✏️ Read and complete. Draw.

I'm _____ .

I'm at home in
the kitchen. I like

_____ ,

but I don't like

_____ .

My favorite food is

_____ .

Me!

93

Grammar reference

9 Order the words.

① can   sing.   He   _____

② They   swim.   can't   _____

③ Can   ride a bike?   you   _____

10 Look and complete.

| am   not   Are   Are |

① _____ you flying your plane?   Yes, I _____ .

② _____ you playing the guitar?   No, I'm _____ .

11 Circle the sentences.

What'shedoing?Heistakingabath.Ishereading?

12 Look and complete.

| like   don't like |

① ☺ I _____ cake.

② ☹ I _____ ice cream.

Wild animals (page 53)

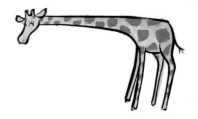  

 # My clothes (page 59)

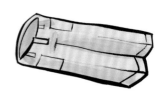  

Fun time! (page 69)

At the amusement park (page 75)

Our house (page 83)

Party time! (page 89)